Nights at the Calcutta Café

edited by

Peter Schulman
and
Somrita Urni Ganguly

Finishing Line Press
Georgetown, Kentucky

Nights at the Calcutta Café

ACKNOWLEDGMENTS

For Ali the owner of the original Calcutta Café in New York.
Many thanks to Les Editions Noroît for allowing for our translation of
Hector Ruiz's "Missing Dog."

Publisher: Leah Huete de Maines
Editor: Christen Kincaid
Cover Art: Peter Schulman
Author Photos: Peter Schulman: Muriel Singer
              Somrita Urni Ganguly: Smeetha Bhoumik
Cover Design: Elizabeth Maines McCleavy

Order online: www.finishinglinepress.com
            also available on amazon.com

Author inquiries and mail orders:
Finishing Line Press
PO Box 1626
Georgetown, Kentucky 40324
USA

Table of Contents

Based on
"Nights at the Calcutta Café" Online Poetry Reading Session
(December 28, 2020)

Curated by
Peter Schulman
Naina Dey

Calcutta Café: Preface

The title of this collection comes from a little and now erstwhile Indian restaurant that used to bless the upper-west side of Manhattan near Columbia University with its intimacy, warmth, and idiosyncratic dishes created by its owner Ali. One dish in particular, a spicy Indian take on the Indonesian *Nasi Goreng* would cause me such cravings that long after I had graduated from Columbia and left New York altogether, I would take the M60 bus from Laguardia Airport directly to the restaurant (its last stop) so that not a minute would go by before I could be reunited with my favorite meal. As the years went by, Ali could be seen standing by one of the windows of *Calcutta Café,* looking increasingly forlorn as his clientele had dwindled to a precious few loyalists. As a result of accelerating gentrification and the arrival of snazzy, hip Indian newcomers that popped-up along Broadway, the restaurant was often empty and I would usually be the only one luxuriously dining there at times.

In order to "save" his restaurant, I had the idea to create a major poetry series there on "off-nights" which were really most nights. I would focus on Indian poets living in New York and gradually expand to include a wide-variety of local and international poets. I imagined late jazz-club-like nights with the *Calcutta Café* suddenly transformed into a crowded, stimulating literary hub.

Alas, my dream was just that—as one night, when I typically got off the M60 and blindly marched towards my Nasi Goreng, I saw, to my horror, a sign thanking the restaurant's loyal customers with a vague promise of re-opening somewhere else in the not too distant future. The tables all set for imaginary diners with elegant tablecloths, cutlery and goblets remained visible through the restaurant's storefront window like a still-life for almost a year before vanishing for good when a fancy coffee shop eventually took the space over.

I had continued to harbor my original fantasy of launching a series of Indian poetry nights when I met Kolkata poets Nana Dey and Somrita Urni Ganguly and the idea of concretizing my idea into actual nights of poetry in a café in Kolkata emerged. We could gather local poets and visiting poets from around the world we thought. Sadly, with the advent of the pandemic, not only were restaurants shuttered but so were borders, and once again the idea had to remain on hold... until an even better border-breaking virtual café was created through Zoom—with our first-ever "Nights at the Calcutta Café" reading in December 2020 that became a lovely bridge between Kolkata, Norfolk, Montreal, New York and Toronto. The moving poems you will discover in this collection tell of cities, loves, longings, ruins and the human spirit that can not only help us overcome the turmoil of our times but give us hope and inspiration through these mystical nights. While the brick-and-mortar *Calcutta Café* may have disappeared, the power of poetry to construct its own spiritual and elevating new Calcutta Café has only begun.

Peter Schulman
Norfolk, Virginia

A Privileged Glimpse of the Dead
Joanna Eleftheriou

The guns (Turkish, Greek) went quiet in Cyprus;
men went home; Androulla Palma slept alone.
Her husband, a ghost; her island, torn asunder.
Wait for him, the government said.
The Turks! They took him to sweat in their salt mines.
Wait.

Androulla knew (in 1974, after the war)
that the man was dead.
For twenty-odd years Androulla drove
up to the UN men, in baby blue helmets,
down to the suntanned Greek Cypriot villagers,
up to the suntanned Turkish Cypriot guards,
asking for word of her ghost.

At five one morning in August, 1998,
with a fellow Penelope riding shotgun,
Androulla shouldered an axe,
a shovel, snuck into the warriors'
cemetery, and began to hack
at one nameless grave
after the next. Soon,
the women's axes struck bone.
Policemen stopped the Penelopes
mid grave-robbery. At the jail,
policemen questioned,
then set them free. Front-page
stories of black-clad Penelopes
clawing at clavicles, belt buckles,
ribcages, bootlaces, and stones
drove the political men to act.

They hired an American
forensic anthropologist.
With DNA, he'll expose
what the government hid.

1

He'll confirm that the husbands, slain
and left here, in their own city,
have lain (unnamed) for twenty-five years.
It was not, after all, the Turks,
or their salt mines, ravenous for men.
How much blame have we Greeks
heaped, like so much rotting flesh,
on our old enemy? Greek Cypriot political men
sealed the dirty secret under dirt.
How many women must undo
the lawless burials of men?

The American forensic anthropologist
will deliver the bones, state the unflattering facts
(death by friendly fire), and offer, in his words,
a privileged glimpse of the dead,
but not before he laments:
some exhumations took place in the past
by persons who were not professionals.
This, he'll complain, has created complications.

Widows now, and Penelopes no longer,
the women will sing, at last,
a funeral rite. Ghosts will rest.
When an interviewer asks about closure
for Antigone's Speech (a documentary),
Androulla Palma will proclaim:
They've pulled out the knife.
Now, I have only my wound.

lisa it's your birthday; happy birthday lisa
Catherine Cormier-Larose

it was the wood of the counter and then the wooden ravine; what was there and what was not anymore; accepting that things are simply lost sometimes.

images or little phrases hidden in between kitchen plates; pinterest is educating the masses about self-care; self-care is not getting killed every night on the way home.

christmas lights all year round but the set is all blue; blue is the snow and the way it coagulates; working so hard towards being a fucking snowflake.

every single day opening the computer and typing; sentiments are a luxury left at the door; every night the long lost mattress opens up like Moby Dick, a reassurance that the end is near.

walking and spinning and running and swimming; sports are a lie told to youngsters to keep them quiet; don't worry, no one ever lived that long.

watching; not blinking; practicing yoga poses without laughing; even netflix has no idea of the essence of being.

keeping lists; eyeing a gratitude journal with murder envy; only evolving in a second language so as to not mistake the imposter's syndrome for a friend.

trying to read. a festive christmas tree disintegrating on a nearby sidewalk; moving from a hot coffee to another.

home is that place barely affordable every other month; it includes insects, mice, rats, bed bugs but not the heat; keeping the lights out: living the dream.

cooking with what's on hand; boiling water and empty cauldrons and witches' cutlery; keeping the smell of poverty at a minimum is a mastered art.

regretting education; drinks with friends; taking the subway; every move is a loonie away from the truth.

sitting in front of an empty auditorium for hours; scratching compulsively; hiding everything under a jean jacket; continuously texting.

The Girl on the Phone
Somrita Urni Ganguly

I was walking home late last night
Down the cobbled streets of the sour-whisky smelling
Southside of New York City
I had watched a Colombian movie
Spanish with English subs
Mamá
About an estranged mother and her daughter
And her daughter's daughter
And how the three briefly find love
And comfort
And solace in one another
The girl walking ahead of me on the footpath was on the phone
Crying
And after every four or five sentences repeating
How can you do this to me?
How can you leave me alone?

I love people who are unafraid to get drunk
I love sitting down with them
And hearing their drunk stories
There is an honesty in their tears
A vulnerability in their lies
An indiscretion in their warmth and abandon
Even the best of us have to fake
In our best composed moments
And so I followed the slightly drunk deeply
Disturbed girl until
I had to cross the road and walk over to the other side

Have I really been able to go over to the other side?

I thought of my last two breakdowns in the last couple of years
The letters I had written came back unanswered
All sixty-one of them
I seem to have sent them to a wrong address

In my late teens and early twenties
I never cried when the men came and went
I was confident and brave and uncaring
I had the kind of arrogance that comes with youth
They could leave but I knew they would come back someday
And even if they didn't others would
But by the time I approached thirty I lost that faith in them
And in me
And so I cried the last two times they left
On the phone
Like that girl repeating
How can you do this to me?
How can you leave me alone?

I wanted to stop the girl on the road
Shake her up and say
We need to be young again
We need to be shameless
Reck
   less
Brave
Hopeful
There are too many of us unseeing the dreams
We once dared to chase

I wanted to tell the girl
I too had cried on the phone
But the men left anyway
They were meant to leave anyway
You cannot make people stay when they are determined
To go away
My love for those men had been hypothetical ~
Assumptions based on insufficient evidence

I wanted to tell the girl
In the last few months that I have been alone
I did not regret that the men had gone
What I regret is that I humbled myself for them
To love and not be loved in return is fucking brutal
I wanted to tell her
There is no beauty in fighting madly
Maniacally
For love
Where there is none
Some things look good only in the movies
In life they tend to bring hurt and humiliation

I wanted to tell the girl
She needs to apologise to herself
On behalf of those who had not
If a sorry is what you are waiting for
Let me tell you it will not come
If a sorry will help you move on
Say a sorry to yourself
(the one they won't say)
And do move on

I wanted to tell the girl
There is no point in asking
How some people live with themselves
After damaging others' homes
I wanted to tell her
What follows those phone calls to unwilling lovers
Is regret
I regret
That I had cried and begged and pleaded with them to stay

I regret
That my mother never taught me how to live by myself and
How my father and my sister and my neighbour and
My god and my dog and my cat
All
Always spoke of adjustments and compromises
Friendship and love
Prescriptions to a happy life
There was no prescription on how to make it on my own
On how to watch a film by myself alone
In a theatre full of people
On how to order for a three course or
A two course or
A one course or
Any meal at all for myself
In a restaurant alone
Surrounded by cheer and laughter and
Whispered promises and sweet kisses
On how to go to a flea market or
A park or a picnic on a Sunday afternoon alone
On how to live by myself
With myself
On my own
Alone

I wish I could tell the girl
The person she was on the phone with
Would leave anyway
I wish I could tell her
You are not an Airbnb room sister
Where the men can come and go

Your body will not be their holiday destination
Their weekend getaway
Their staycation
You are worth more

I wish I could share with her the prescription
On how to make it on her own

But by the time I got the medication
That girl was long gone

A part of this work was previously published in *Stranger Stories* (USA, 2020).

Missing Dog
Hector Ruiz
Translated from the French by Peter Schulman

Pajamas float in the park
the overflowing ashtrays on the balconies
are no remedy for ennui

between phantoms and witches
randomly I
hang some pumpkins

on the walls of the Davidson my chest expands
when the waitress speaks of her boyfriend
happiness is romantic jealousy

Marcel gives up on his medicine
Audrey mentions the importance of pursuing one's dreams
A lady gives two clementines to the pusher

in the restroom with each dose she brushes against
her broke son's body
love grows in the arms of emptiness

The poem in French, 'Chien perdu,' was published in *Racines et Fictions* (Editions du Noroît, Canada, 2019).

untitled

Catherine Cormier-Larose

1.
we found my dead friend's name
in hot bold pink letters
abandoned on a cleared table

although we tried to steal them back
make them disappear
own them
they stood there

we hope for the best:
un feu de paille

2.
you come from ancestors
violated on all sides
that poked a hole
burnt marks on your shoulders
you're healing like a stove element
i'm sorry i started the fire
you don't know what to do with a pyromaniac

3.
we screamed on the streets
lost a couple along the way
this is how poetry gets made
when we hit sidewalks
our jaws breaking
crashing against the stores' windows
sliding through the sewer drains
burning ourselves on electric tea lights

forgetting to pay the bar tab

4.
i'd watch you sleep if i wasn't always falling asleep first
for once you wouldn't mistake my snoring for waves that could
take you through the night

row row row the boat: water beats fire

5.
you look at my left knee don't worry it will be fine
i want you to know what fine is for me
i want you to keep it in your palms, watch it come and go in
between your fingers

slap me with it the next time we see each other

6.
i can hear the holes in your chest breathing at me
run your fingers through my spine
dislodge my bones, it is fine:
un feu d'artifice

signal

Kelly Norah Drukker

crossing through alleyways
speech is mapped

in a phone through signals
I reach with my voice

ears hurtling toward
the honey of a tone

that catches my words
volleys a story with legs

we build it taller and higher
teetering on the brink

of a laugh that loosens
the throat I search

for your voice through
distance imposed feet

tunnel through snow past
back gardens Christmas

lights strung over ashen
plants leaves still lifting

like paper whipped this quiet
descended so quickly no

time to gather the leaves red
and brimming to harvest

the colour and drink still
to walk through silence

like a furrow ploughed
is to feel it strip you

to marrow narrow
the flute of the soul

to a reed that calls reaches
in the dusk even

when the signal breaks
and the voice is trembling

Down the River Ganga
Naina Dey

Gentle ripples, heavy with silt
Pale as a tinted marble floor
Hiding unfathomable depths below
With a black barge or two
Empty, desolate like giant birds resting afloat
Buoys bobbing
Painted crimson
Distinct dots on the dusty horizon

Brick kilns line the banks
Smoking chimneys
Like pillars of dying embers
Naked boys frolic
Sending up sprays of droplets innumerable
On the steps an old man at his late ablution

A watery expanse
Perturbed only by the cool breeze
Sprinkled with gold dust of the noonday sun
When towers like a vision wonderful the earthly abode
Of the Divine Mother of Dakshineshwar
The dark deity cocooned by her majestic shrine
As safe as a seed inside fleshy fruit
The soul of a city of teeming multitudes
Silent yet omnipresent
As the river that flows languidly by.

Relocation
Gopal Lahiri

Time is not still, it recounts an uprooting, a discovery.
The evening speaks unfamiliar words, a sudden fury comes over,

turn to the rain again,
flow has become a torrent now.

Sitting on the top of a wild date palm,
the crescent moon

can't disentangle itself from the raging clouds.
The banks are the lurking shadows, the boats

in the middle, toss and bump, rock and roll,
begin to dissolve.

The stormy wind charges in with a faint hiss,
imparting a gloss to its rawness.

Wave after wave,
full of scary eddies and swirls,

tides swell, grown into high-decibel songs.
Missing faces gather, drained of colour, crumble,

begging unconditional shelter,
For there is much death here as well as life.

First published in *International Journal on Multicultural Literature*
(January 2021).

Park Street
Amit Shankar Saha

A blue gypsy skirt seeks
hollow beings in Park Street.
Colours of countdown
stop the traffic of time.
At the book store
no dumb-waiters wait
for requisitions of memory.
At the eateries
queue chunks of cosmos.
So many nebulas
drown in the Olypubs.
There is no abracadabra
in the black holes I bring
to the galaxy in Park Street.

First published in *Balconies of Time* (India, 2017).

I, Earth

Mallika Sengupta
Translated from the Bangla by Catherine Fletcher

Oh yes, I am Mother Earth:
floods born from my blood,
oozing firebomb,
sludge, musk of a wondrous planet.
At birth she declared, I am your mother.
Yet, who came first—was it Earth or was it Woman?
Was it Woman or fathomless Earth?

Perhaps it's all so inconceivable.
Perhaps I am this world's daughter,
created by miraculous union of Earth and Sun,
fused from X and Y chromosomes.
I am primordial, limitless, audacious,
born again and again, driven by visions.
Within me I have nurtured this planet's every atom.

Earth and I are sometimes sisters,
sometimes mother, sometimes daughter.
Quietly within in our blood,
love thus grows rapturous.
We live on entangled with one another
Mothers, daughters, sisters:
Earth and I.

First published in *Rattapallax* Vol. 21 (2013); reprinted here with the permission of Mallika Sengupta's estate and Subodh Sarkar.

Park Street
Sanjukta Dasgupta

"That school on Park Street is so beautiful"
The awestruck student told her teacher
The nun of her missionary school replied
"we are all missionaries
But their school is for the rich
Our school is for the poor"
The student rushed back to her parents
"Our school is for the poor, sister said
Who are rich, what do they do
I know they read the same books
Do the same exams as we do
But they must be dressed in silks in summer
Eating biriyani all the time"

No buses plied on Park Street
No rickshaws, the chariots of fire
No bicycles, no hawkers
Bystanders and busy pedestrians
Lined the pavements stretched
In front of magic names and heavy doors
Guards guarded those doors that swung open
For the rich, slammed shut for the poor
No parking on Park Street for the poor
It was a seductive street that ravished the rich
And humiliated the poor!

First published in *Sita's Sisters* (India, 2019).

Love during Covid-19

Naina Dey

Let me imagine the end of the world
Monuments falling and you and me
Running running
Beautifully disheveled in denim
Past screaming people, cars crashing
Until we enter a blasted street
To steal a kiss
Let me imagine men and women
Gasping for breath
Ourselves bruised and shaken in the right proportion
An empty house
Hot bath, bed, wine and candles
For us only
Like in the films
As I stand a meter apart
Masked and gloved
I despair for the last pouch of milk
Thinking about next day's meal
Fish or not
While you forage for you and yours
In the wilderness of social distancing
Love is for TV in good times
And fake apocalypses

Some Place Else
Amit Shankar Saha

Last night you
at Someplace Else,
having a drink
with a friend.
Tonight I
drink a spirit
of unrequitedness,
glass shivers at my sip.
Is this the rim
that touched your lips?
Under the surface
of my spirit
a farmer boy
tries to speak.
His mouth filled
with dead snakes,
his eyes swell
and swim with loss.
Waiter, please,
how much my drink cost?

First published in *Balconies of Time* (India, 2017).

Spotlight

Gopal Lahiri

Morning is still unborn,

Cloudy curtains like crushed sarees disappear
after the rain,

The sky is now awash with
hope and innocence,

A row of spotlights nails to the boundary wall,
stone lamp glows in front of the Kalighat temple,
removing darkness,
the city is at its most beaming, noiseless,

Festoons hang on the doorway
tramlines draw the traffic pattern.

The green leaves hide
against the silhouette of trees,
the wilted bakul withers, longing for sunlight,

Somewhere a tiny voice cracks
the first sound,

Morning has never been such a restless infant.

First published in *From Prinsep Ghat to Pir Panjal* (ebook, 2021).

Translation

Lost in translation?
Sanjukta Dasgupta

When we met
Our mutual words transcended
Transformed in translation
We strung words like pearls
Mother tongue and Other tongue
A new poem born out of the womb
Of a well-known old poem
The original home-grown poem
Became a global sapling
Rooted, uprooted, re-rooted
Unique avatar
Linguistic transfer
Cultural code switching
Those are puzzles for sages
And heat oppressed brains
Ethnic poems in global syntax
Global poems in ethnic inscription
Smiled in the new dawn
Reaching hearts and minds
Liberated from the intense entrapment
In either/or- singular tongues
Our willing translations
Our mutual spinning of words
In an Other tongue, in our mother tongue
To fill the gaps others hadn't bridged
Insularity and isolation were erased
A rainbow of words
Not a chaotic Babel
Brought us together
Isolated islands of words
Converged into continents of communion

We never regretted any loss in translation
We were incorrigible dreamers, for us

Territories and borders were life- threatening
We dreamt about bringing together
A fractured world with our healing words-
Vasudhaiva Kutumbakum
Our world as a single family
In translation
We gained an inclusive world
We mingled diversity and difference
In our several tongues and daring dreams
We translated uninhibited
For us, to be transfixed and immobile
Was surrender and suicide
We translated and translated and translated
And our mutual words
Became universal symbols, signs and signposts
Our adhesive translations made the Other our own
Fused into a holistic dream come true
Translated, we became indivisible
Not you and me, but us.

First published in *Lakshmi Unbound* (India, 2017).

Editors & Curators:

Dr. Peter Schulman is Professor of French and International Studies at Old Dominion University. He is the author of *The Sunday of Fiction: The Modern French Eccentric* (Purdue UP, 2003) as well as *Le Dernier Livre du Siècle* (Romillat, 2001) with Mischa Zabotin. He has translated Jules Verne's last novel *The Secret of Wilhelm Storitz*; George Simenon's *The 13 Culprits* as well as a meditation on waves by Marie Darrieussecq, *On Waves; Suburban Beauty* from poet Jacques Reda; *Adamah* from poet Celine Zins; Ying Chen's collection of haiku *Impressions of Summer* and Silvia Baron Supervielle's *Pages of Travel*. He is currently co-editor in chief of a journal of eco-criticism, *Green Humanities* with Josh Weinstein and has co-edited the following books: *The Marketing of Eros: Performance, Sexuality and Consumer Culture* (2003); *Chasing Esther: Jewish Expressions of Cultural Difference* (2006) and *Rhine Crossings: France and German in Love and War* (SUNY Press, 2005).

Dr. Naina Dey teaches at Maharaja Manindra Chandra College. She is a critic, translator and a widely anthologised creative writer. She has authored several books on critical studies, and her publications include two volumes of poetry titled *Snapshots from Space and Other Poems* and *Homing Pigeons and Sundry Stuff*. She was member of the jury for the International Poetry Chapbook Contest 2018 organised by Rhythm Divine Poets, Kolkata, and a festival delegate representing Intercultural Poetry and Performance Library at the Apeejay Kolkata Literary Festival 2019. She was awarded the "Excellence in World Poetry Award, 2009" by the International Poets Academy, Chennai, and was among a team of young Indian writers to be felicitated jointly by Sahitya Akademi and Visva-Bharati University in 2010. Of her latest publications are a translation of Upendrakishore Ray Chowdhury's "Gupi Gain O Bagha Bain" and *One Dozen Stories*, a book of short story translations. She is concept creator of literary and artistic organ Chamunda's Dream.

Dr. Somrita Urni Ganguly is a professor, poet, and literary translator. She was a Fulbright Doctoral Fellow at Brown University, USA, and is currently Head of the Department of English, Maharaja Manindra Chandra College, University of Calcutta. Dr. Ganguly has served as a judge for the PEN America Translation Prize, and an Expert Reader for the English PEN Translation Grant, the National Translation Award (USA), and the National Endowment for the Arts Translation Grant offered by the US federal government. Somrita co-founded The Writing Programme in collaboration with leading publishers such as Simon & Schuster and Pan Macmillan. Her work has been showcased at the London Book Fair, and she has read in cities like Bloomington, Bombay, Boston, Calcutta, Cove, Delhi, Hyderabad, London, Miami, Providence, and Singapore. Somrita edited the first anthology of food poems, *Quesadilla and Other Adventures* (2019), and has translated *Firesongs* (2019), *Shakuni: Master of the Game* (2019), and *The Midnight Sun: Love Lyrics and Farewell Songs* (2018), among other works.

Contributors:

Catherine Cormier-Larose is the author of *L'avion est un reflexe court* (Del Buso, 2017) and *Anthologie de la poésie actuelle des femmes au Québec* with Vanessa Bell (Remue Mégae, 2021). She is co-artistic and managing director of La Maison de la Poésie de Montréal and the Festival de la Poésie de Montréal (FPM).

Dr. Sanjukta Dasgupta, Professor and Former Head, Department of English, and Former Dean, Faculty of Arts, Calcutta University, has been the recipient of the Fulbright postdoctoral fellowship and Fulbright Scholar in Residence grant. She received the IWSFF Women Achievers Award, Kolkata in 2019 and the WE Kamala Das Poetry Award in 2020. Dasgupta is a poet, short story writer, critic and translator, and has 21 authored/ edited published books.

Kelly Norah Drukker is a Montreal-based writer. Her poetry collection Small Fires (MQUP, 2016) won the A.M. Klein Prize for Poetry and the Concordia University First Book Prize, and was a finalist for the Grand Prix du livre de Montréal. Petits feux (trans. Lori Saint-Martin, Paul Gagné) appeared in 2018.

Joanna Eleftheriou is the author of the essay *collection This Way Back*. She has published essays and poems in *Arts & Letters, Assay,* and *Sweeter Voices Still: An LGBTQ Anthology from Middle America*. An alumna of Old Dominion University, Joanna teaches at Christopher Newport University and is a language teacher at the Writing Workshops in Greece.

Catherine Fletcher is a poet and playwright. Her recent work has appeared or is forthcoming in *The Hopper, Kissing Dynamite, Hopkins Review, Burning House Press*, and the concert series Concept Lab. She was a TWP Science and Religion Fellow at Arizona State University, served as Director of Poetry Programs at the New York-based organization City Lore, and Managing Director of the Los Angeles-based ensemble The Ghost Road Company. For more, visit http:// cafletcher.blogspot.com.

Gopal Lahiri was born and lives in Kolkata, India. He is a bilingual poet, writer, editor, critic and translator and has published in English and Bengali. He has 23 published books to his credit. His works have been published in various journals and anthologies worldwide, and translated into 14 languages.

Hector Ruiz is the author of *Racines et Fictions* (2019); *Taverne nationale* (2019) with Domininic Marcil; *Lire la rue, marcher le poème* (2016) with Dominic Marcil; *Gestes domestiques* (2011) and *Délier les rues* (2018).

Amit Shankar Saha is the author of three collections of poems titled *Balconies of Time, Fugitive Words,* and *Illicit Poe*ms. A Pushcart Prize, Griffin Poetry Prize, and Best of Net nominee, he has a PhD in English from Calcutta University and teaches at Seacom Skills University. His website is www.amitshankarsaha.com.

Mallika Sengupta (1960-2011) was a proponent of an unapologetically political poetry and an important voice in contemporary Bengali literature. She began writing in 1981, published eleven books of poetry, two novels and several essays, and edited an anthology of women's poetry from Bengal. She was the head of the Department of Sociology in Maharani Kasiswari College, University of Calcutta, and Poetry Editor of *Sananda*, a Bengali women's fortnightly. For more, see www. poetryinternational.org/pi/poet/2728/Mallika-Sengupta/en/tile.